DK SUPERGUIDES
ICE SKATING

The Kilian hold

The takeoff for a toe loop

Parallel spin

The landing position for all jumps

DK SUPERGUIDES
ICE SKATING

Written by Peter Morrissey
Foreword by Todd Eldredge

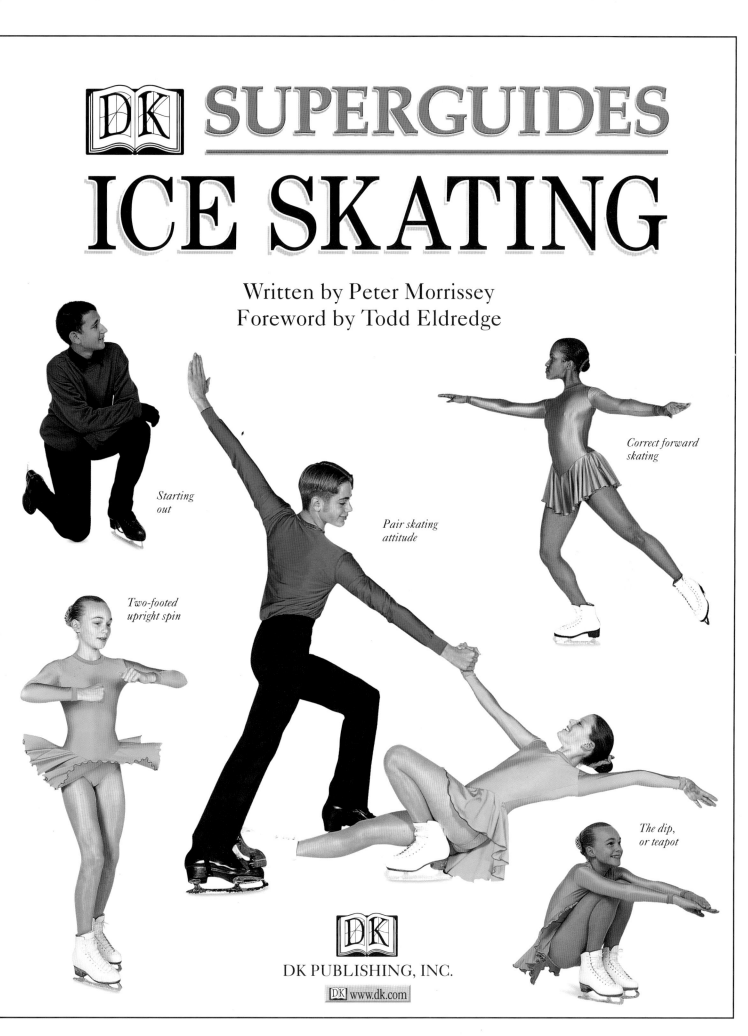

Starting out

Pair skating attitude

Correct forward skating

Two-footed upright spin

The dip, or teapot

DK PUBLISHING, INC.

www.dk.com

DK

A DORLING KINDERSLEY BOOK

DK www.dk.com

Project editor Fiona Robertson **Project art editor** Rebecca Johns
Editor Elinor Greenwood
Photography Andy Crawford
DTP Designer Almudena Díaz and Nicky Studdart
Picture researchers Andrea Sadler and Maureen Sheerin
Production Orla Creegan

The young ice skaters
Zoia Birmingham, Shellie Gee, Adam Goudie
Louisa Hicks, Phillip Poole, John Wright

First American Edition, 2000
2 4 6 8 10 9 7 5 3 1

Published in the United States by
Dorling Kindersley Publishing, Inc.
95 Madison Avenue
New York, NY 10016

ISBN: 0-7894-5427-0

Color reproduction by Colourscan, Singapore
Printed and bound in Italy by L.E.G.O.

Contents

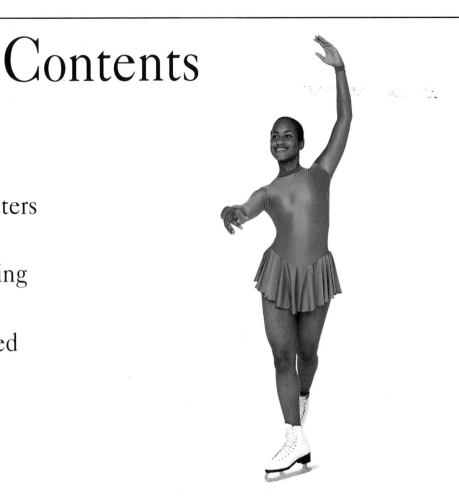

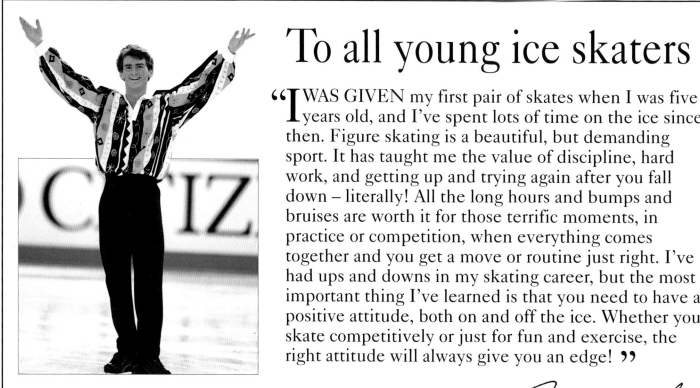

To all young ice skaters

"**I** WAS GIVEN my first pair of skates when I was five years old, and I've spent lots of time on the ice since then. Figure skating is a beautiful, but demanding sport. It has taught me the value of discipline, hard work, and getting up and trying again after you fall down – literally! All the long hours and bumps and bruises are worth it for those terrific moments, in practice or competition, when everything comes together and you get a move or routine just right. I've had ups and downs in my skating career, but the most important thing I've learned is that you need to have a positive attitude, both on and off the ice. Whether you skate competitively or just for fun and exercise, the right attitude will always give you an edge! **"**

"Medaling in a competition is one of the most exhilarating experiences a skater can have. Here, I'm celebrating a silver medal at the 1995 World Figure Skating Championships."

"I won a gold medal at Skate America 1995. This victory was especially sweet because it came on my home turf – my training town, Detriot, Michigan."

"I try to make every moment on the ice count. This short program helped me win first place in the 1998 US Figure Skating Championships."

"Skating moves like this require balance, grace, and precision. You've got to be strong and focused, but don't forget to have fun! The best skaters look and feel at home on the ice."

"No matter where you place, representing your country and your sport in the Olympic Games is a thrilling honor."

History of ice skating

Early Viking boot skate
Experts believe that the earliest skates were splinters of bone attached to boots, like this Viking boot from the 10th century. People probably used poles to move forward.

Prince Albert's skate
Ice skating was extremely popular with the aristocracy and the Royal Family. This ornate metal skate dates from 1851, and was worn by Prince Albert.

Queen Victoria's skate
Queen Victoria also enjoyed ice skating. Her skates date from 1854 and were made from metal, wood, and leather. They would have been crafted to fit her foot exactly.

Palais de Glace
By 1926, skating had become very popular all over the world. The world-famous Palais de Glace ice rink was on the Champs Elysées in Paris, France.

SKATING ON ICE began many hundreds of years ago as a means of transportation. The word "skate" comes from the Dutch word meaning leg shank, or bone, and the earliest skates were probably splinters of bone fixed to boots. Skating as we know it today began at the end of the 19th century, with American skater Jackson Haines. His balletlike movements were very different from the stiff, precise style of English skating. A combination of the two styles gave rise to the international style of skating we know today.

Early transportation
At the beginning of the 20th century in Holland, skating along frozen canals in winter was a quick and fun method of transportation.

Princess skating rink
The first indoor artificial ice rink opened in England in 1876. Many more rinks opened soon after this, including the Princess Ice Rink in London, above. Skating quickly became a fashionable and popular pastime.

Sonja Henie (1912-69)
The future of women's skating was altered forever by the Norwegian World Champion Figure Skater, Sonja Henie. Henie changed the way female ice skaters dressed, their boots, and their style on the ice. She brought ice skating to the masses and became the most famous female skater of all time.

Skating outdoors
Many of the first World Championships were held at outdoor rinks, such as this one at St. Moritz in Switzerland. These skaters are performing an exhibition event in the 1930s.

Pair skaters
In the 1960s, Russian pair skaters Ludmila and Oleg Protopopov introduced an artistic style of pair skating that had never been seen before. They created many new moves, including the "death spiral," which pair skaters today include in their skating programs.

What you will need

WHEN YOU FIRST start skating, your priority is to be warm and comfortable. Wear a sweat suit or even a skisuit on the ice and always wear gloves for safety. As you become more advanced, you may want to wear practical, attractive outfits that let you move more freely, and emphasize excellent body lines. Rent some skates from your local ice rink at first, then if you decide that skating is for you, you can buy your own from a specialized store.

A simple skating dress made from a stretch material will show off your body line, which is very important in skating.

Girls' equipment
Most girls wear skating dresses, or skirts with T-shirts or leotards and warm tights. Your outfit should be comfortable and practical for the ice. Girls usually wear white boots.

Ice skates
The most important piece of skating equipment is your ice skates. The skates consist of a boot, which is usually leather, and a blade. Your boots must fit properly, which means that they should be snug yet relatively comfortable, and provide good support for your ankles.

Leather boot

Toe pick

Blade

The sleeves of your outfit should be quite tight at the wrists.

Laces can be cotton or an elastic mixture.

You should wear blade protectors (guards) at all times off the ice.

The skirt lets you move freely while you skate.

Whitener will help keep your boots very clean.

Blades
There are different blades for different types of skating. The blades are made of steel and must be kept dry and well protected, or they will rust. All blades have two edges (see pages 22–23), and should be re-sharpened, or ground, on a regular basis.

An ice-dance blade

A free-skating blade

You can wear either flesh-colored tights, or tights that match your outfit.

A strong skating bag will keep your equipment safe and protected.

Gloves
Gloves are a very important part of your equipment. As a beginner, wear gloves to keep your hands warm and to protect them when you fall. You can buy gloves to match your outfits. Always carry a spare pair with you.

Your boots should fit your feet perfectly. Never buy or rent boots that are too big.

Boys usually like to wear simple outfits, such as this one.

Ice rink

Ice rinks cater to the general public in addition to holding private sessions for club skaters and advanced competitive skaters. Many ice rinks hold "Learn to Skate" and "Fun Skate" sessions, which will teach you how to skate properly. Your local ice rink will also have fully qualified skating coaches who can give you private instruction and teach you the correct techniques. Most ice rinks have a pro shop where you can buy all the equipment you need. Before you go skating, find out the most suitable times for your level.

During practice sessions, wear a sweatshirt over your outfit to keep warm.

Lacing up

Correctly laced boots are the most important part of ice skating and will make your sessions more pleasurable.

1 Place your foot into the boot and lace the boot up from your toes to the base of your ankle.

2 Your boots must be firmly laced at the base of your ankle, as this area needs the most support. Keep your foot upright while lacing.

You can wear sweat suit bottoms or stretch pants.

An elastic stirrup that fastens under your boots will ensure a good leg line.

Pair skating

If you skate with a partner, it is important that you wear matching outfits, even in practice. This not only looks good, but also helps you feel like part of a couple. Special designers can make costumes that match perfectly.

Boys' equipment

Boys should look sharp on the ice. They usually wear skating pants made of stretch material, which make it easier to move and bend, and loose- or tight-fitting tops. For practice, many boys wear a sweat suit and T-shirt. Most boys wear black boots.

Boys usually wear black boots.

3 Tie your laces in a double knot at the top and keep them short. They should be firm, but not too tight.

Warming up

BEFORE YOU BEGIN any skating session, you should always warm up, both off and on the ice. Warming up is essential for helping to reduce the risk of injury while you skate, and also makes your skating more fun. Try some of the exercises shown here to increase your flexibility, body temperature, range of movement, and heart rate.

Lunge

To increase the flexibility in your legs, practice lunging, both on and off the ice. Keep your back straight and your head up. You should feel a stretch in the muscles at the back of your outstretched leg (the hamstrings).

Rest your hands on your thigh for balance.

Feel the stretch in the back of your leg.

Make sure your knee does not go over your toes.

Neck stretch

It is always a good idea to start your warm up with your head, and work downward. Always do neck exercises slowly and carefully.

1 Stand in a comfortable position with your feet slightly apart and your shoulders relaxed. Face forward.

2 Roll your head slowly to the right and feel a stretch on the left side of your neck.

3 Let your head drop slowly to the front; never force it. Feel a stretch in the back of your neck.

4 Bring your head up and let it roll slowly to the left. Feel the stretch on the right side.

Hip rotations

Rotating the hips and upper body will warm and stretch your hips, lower back, and stomach (abdominal) muscles.

Lean forward as you rotate your hips backward.

Keep looking straight ahead and try to move just your hips, not the rest of your body.

Place your hands on your hips.

Feel the stretch in your right side as you rotate to the right.

Your feet should be flat on the floor.

1 Stand with feet apart and place your hands on your hips. Push your hips to the left and lean to your right.

2 Lean forward slightly and rotate your hips. As your hips move back, you should feel a stretch in your lower back.

3 Rotate your hips around to your right side and feel the stretch in your right side. Keep rotating your hips.

Hamstring stretch

This stretch will warm the muscles at the back of your legs (the hamstrings) and in your thighs (the quadriceps).

1 Sit on the floor with your legs stretched out in front of you.

2 Take your left leg and cross it over your right leg. Place your right foot flat on the floor.

Stretch this arm and shoulder out behind you.

3 Hold on to your left leg and twist your body around to the right. Stretch your right arm and shoulder out behind you. Repeat on the other side.

Hold your leg below your knee.

Box splits

Increase your flexibility with box splits, but be careful not to overstretch at first!

1 Sit on the floor with your back straight. Open both legs as far as possible.

Reach forward.

2 Slowly reach forward with both arms and try to touch the floor in front of you.

3 Rotate to the left and bring your body down over your leg.

Look down at your knees.

Point your toes.

Side rotations

Loosen up your shoulders and back with side rotations. Try to hold each position for about 10 seconds.

1 Face forward and slowly rotate the upper body to the right.

Breathe easy
Try to breathe normally when you stretch; never hold your breath!

Bend your arms and bring them up to shoulder height.

2 Bring your body back to the front. Your feet should not move throughout.

Twist from your waist.

Fingers are touching.

3 Rotate your body to the left. Your hips and legs should face forward.

Jump rope for about 5–10 minutes.

Jump rope
Jumping rope is an excellent way of developing stamina in a confined space. It really increases your heart rate and also helps raise your body temperature.

Keep your breathing regular as you jump.

Arm circling

This exercise loosens the muscles in your arms and shoulders. When combined with stretching upward and bending down, it also works your legs. Make sure you keep your back straight the whole time.

1 Stand with your feet slightly apart, your shoulders relaxed, and your arms stretched out in front of you.

Your arms should be at shoulder height.

Keep your legs slightly bent; don't lock your knees.

2 Keep your arms stretched out and slowly start to bend down. Lift your heels off the floor as you do so.

Use your arms to help you balance.

Keep your arms straight.

3 Come up onto the tips of your toes and lift both arms above your head.

4 Take your arms as far back as they will go to complete the circle. Lower your feet back down on the floor.

Balance on the tips of your toes.

Cooling down
Make sure that you stretch lightly after your skating session, too. This will help prevent aching muscles the next day!

First steps

ONCE YOUR BOOTS are correctly laced and you are wearing warm clothes, you are ready to take your first steps on the ice. You may want to practice walking on the floor in your boots first.

This helps you get used to balancing on thin blades before you move onto the slippery ice. It also helps you practice standing correctly over your skates, which is crucial to your progression as a skater.

Stepping onto the ice

Before you step onto the ice, you must remove the skate guards from your blades. Hold onto the barrier with your right hand and step sideways onto the ice with your left leg. Bring your right foot down onto the ice and place your feet in a "V" position ready to begin. Stretch your arms out in front of you to help you balance, then carefully move away from the edge of the rink.

First steps

When you first step onto the ice, your movements will be slow and you will find it difficult to build up speed. Hold your arms out to the side and slightly in front of you to help you balance.

1 Stand tall with your head up and your arms out to the sides. Place your skates in a "V" position.

2 Bend your knees and lift your left skate up about 2 in (5 cm) off the ice.

3 Place your left foot back on the ice, slightly in front of the right foot.

4 Repeat the same movements with the other leg. Try to keep your upper body still.

5 Continue taking small marching steps forward until you feel confident gliding along.

Falling safely

No one wants to fall on the cold, hard ice, but falling is an inevitable part of learning to skate. It is important that you know how to fall and how to get up quickly and safely. When you begin, you should always wear gloves to keep your hands warm and to protect you from other skaters when you fall.

Taking a tumble
When you are first learning to skate, expect to fall and don't be embarrassed. Falling shows you are pushing yourself to achieve greater things.

2 Lower your center of gravity by bending at the waist. Bend your knees to help break the fall and try to land on your side or bottom.

Keep your hands in front of your body.

Quickly bring your arms and hands toward you to avoid any accidents with other skaters.

Put your hands out to break the fall.

1 When you feel yourself starting to fall, try to relax and let yourself fall forward. This hurts less than falling backward and is not as dangerous.

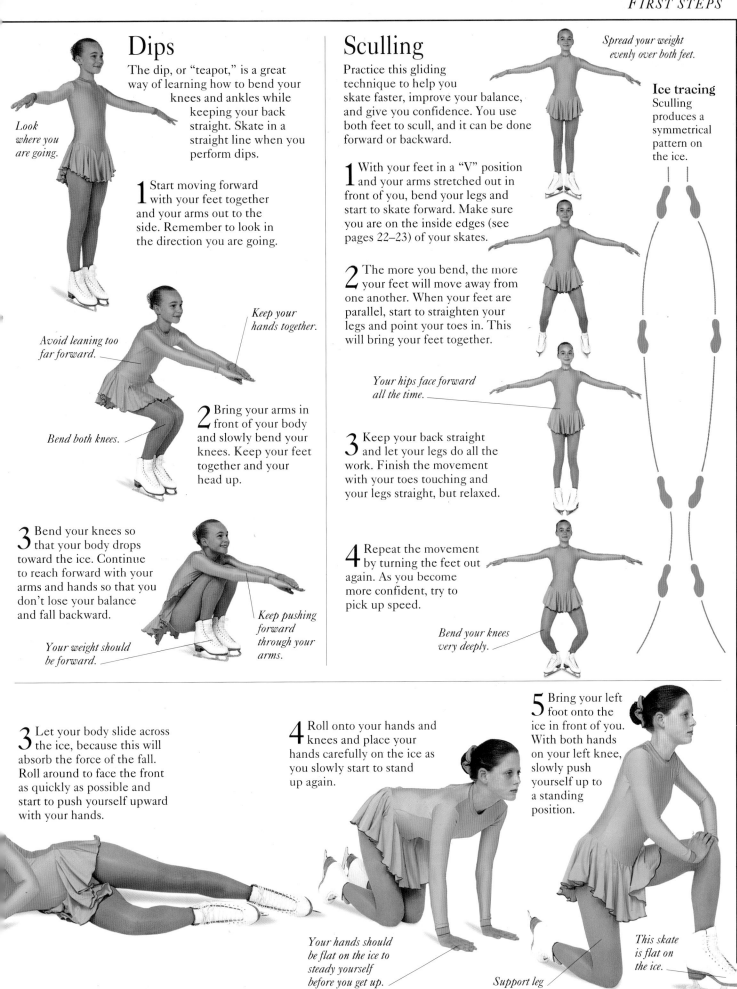

Dips

Look where you are going.

The dip, or "teapot," is a great way of learning how to bend your knees and ankles while keeping your back straight. Skate in a straight line when you perform dips.

1 Start moving forward with your feet together and your arms out to the side. Remember to look in the direction you are going.

Avoid leaning too far forward.

Keep your hands together.

Bend both knees.

2 Bring your arms in front of your body and slowly bend your knees. Keep your feet together and your head up.

3 Bend your knees so that your body drops toward the ice. Continue to reach forward with your arms and hands so that you don't lose your balance and fall backward.

Your weight should be forward.

Keep pushing forward through your arms.

Sculling

Practice this gliding technique to help you skate faster, improve your balance, and give you confidence. You use both feet to scull, and it can be done forward or backward.

1 With your feet in a "V" position and your arms stretched out in front of you, bend your legs and start to skate forward. Make sure you are on the inside edges (see pages 22–23) of your skates.

2 The more you bend, the more your feet will move away from one another. When your feet are parallel, start to straighten your legs and point your toes in. This will bring your feet together.

Your hips face forward all the time.

3 Keep your back straight and let your legs do all the work. Finish the movement with your toes touching and your legs straight, but relaxed.

4 Repeat the movement by turning the feet out again. As you become more confident, try to pick up speed.

Bend your knees very deeply.

Spread your weight evenly over both feet.

Ice tracing
Sculling produces a symmetrical pattern on the ice.

3 Let your body slide across the ice, because this will absorb the force of the fall. Roll around to face the front as quickly as possible and start to push yourself upward with your hands.

4 Roll onto your hands and knees and place your hands carefully on the ice as you slowly start to stand up again.

5 Bring your left foot onto the ice in front of you. With both hands on your left knee, slowly push yourself up to a standing position.

Your hands should be flat on the ice to steady yourself before you get up.

Support leg

This skate is flat on the ice.

Skating forward

L EARNING TO skate forward is
complex because there are so many
things to remember. You have to be able
to skate forward, master forward crossovers, and learn the different stops that
can be done on ice. These moves form the
basis of every other move you will learn in
skating, so you need to perfect them.

*Keep your arms up
to help your balance.*

*Relax your
shoulders.*

2 Push off onto
an outside edge
and start to skate a
curve. Stretch
your free leg
behind you
and turn it
out.

Feet first
Place your feet at
right angles, ready
for the push. Use
the inside edge of
the pushing foot,
not the toe pick.

*Bend both
knees deeply.*

Skating forward

When you skate forward, your movements should
look effortless and flowing, each one progressing
smoothly into the next. It is important to use
graceful knee actions and keep your free leg well
stretched out. Relax your shoulders, hold your
head high, and always look where you are going.

1 Begin with
the heels of
your skates
together. Bring
the right side of
your body
slightly forward.

Crossovers

Mastering crossovers enables
you to skate smoothly around
corners, circles, and in both
directions. Each crossover
consists of two steps and two
pushes. The first step is on
an outside edge; the second
is on an inside edge.

2 Push off onto an
outside edge and
start to skate a curve.
Stretch your free leg
and turn it out.

3 Slowly bring
your free leg
forward. Don't rush
the crossover and
make sure that your
skating foot is still
on the outside edge.
Lean into the curve.

*Lean into
the curve.*

1 Begin with your
feet in the basic
start position for
forward skating.
Your left leg and
right arm should be
pushed out in front.

*Make sure your right skate
is on an inside edge.*

9 When you have completed the
crossover, your right skate should
be on the inside edge and you will be
skating around on a curve.

*Try to keep your
back straight
all the time.*

8 As you bring
your free leg
forward, try to stay
balanced on your
outside edge.

Ice tracing
During each crossover, always ensure
that you have crossed your
feet fully.

*Point your
free foot.*

4 Cross your right leg over
your left leg and place your
right foot onto the ice on an
inside edge. The left skate
will start to push away with
the outside edge, and your leg
will extend backward.

*Keep your
right arm
forward.*

*Return to the
feet-together
position.*

*Inside
edge*

5 Your hips, arms,
and shoulders
should stay in the
same position
throughout. Slowly
bring your feet back
together to start the
crossover again.

6 Make sure you
bend your knees
before you push off
again. This adds power
to your movement and
stops you from using
your toe pick.

7 Bend
your
skating leg
and stretch
the free leg
out behind
you as you
glide.

*Stretch out
your free leg.*

Make sure you push with the full blade, and from an inside edge.

As you close your feet, the left side of your body will come forward slightly.

Bring the new skating side of your body forward.

Avoid lunging forward with every step; make your actions smooth.

3 Transfer your body weight from the pushing foot onto the skating foot, and you will find yourself gliding forward.

4 Try to hold the glide on the outside edge for as long as possible, before slowly closing your feet.

5 Bend your knees and push off on the opposite leg. Open your pushing foot fully so that the push can take place cleanly from the inside edge.

Always stretch and point your free foot.

Concentrate on bending the skating knee to get a strong push.

6 Keep the new skating leg bent and your free leg extended behind you and turned out. Your new skating foot is on an outside edge.

Practice It is important for you to skate forward properly, so practice every time you skate.

Stopping

Once you have learned how to skate forward, it is important you learn how to stop correctly. There are three main stopping movements – the snowplow, which is the easiest, the "T" stop, and the hockey stop, which is quite advanced.

Your shoulders and hips should face the front.

Transfer your body weight onto the back foot.

Extend your free leg behind you.

1 The "T" stop is a difficult stop to control, but looks very elegant when it is done properly. Begin by skating along in a straight line on one foot. Remember to look where you are going.

2 Slowly bring your free leg down toward the skating foot. Place your free foot on the ice on an outside edge, just behind the skating foot. Keep your feet in this "T" position as you come to a stop.

Feet first At the end of the stop, your back foot should be well turned out and on an outside edge.

Snowplow

Most skaters learn the snowplow stop first because it is quite easy to pick up. However, it does require a lot of practice to master it correctly.

Look straight ahead of you.

Keep your body under control.

Arms stretched out

1 Begin by skating along in a straight line with your knees bent and your skates on their inside edges.

Hockey stop

This dynamic stop is also known as the parallel stop. You have to control your hips, shoulders, and arms, and the inside and outside edges of your skates.

1 Skate forward on both feet in a straight line. Practice turning to the right and the left to see which side you prefer.

2 Bend both knees deeply. If you turn to the left, your left foot should be on an outside edge and your right foot on an inside edge.

Face forward all the time.

3 Straighten up, quickly turn both skates to the left, and bend your knees again.

Your body is facing forward.

Turn your heels out.

Your arms should stay absolutely still.

2 Keep your knees bent as you gradually push the feet apart and turn your toes inward.

Skating backward

O NCE YOU HAVE learned to skate forward, it is time to tackle skating backward. Skating backward requires a great deal of patience and hard work and will feel very strange at first because you cannot see where you are going. However, it is the most efficient way of gaining speed and, once you have mastered the basic techniques, it's also great fun!

Backward crossovers

When you can skate backward confidently, you can progress to backward crossovers. You should learn to do these in a circle, or part of a circle, and in both directions.

Face into the circle.

Your arms are level and stretched out.

Bend your knees deeply as you push off.

Free leg

1 Face into the circle. Push off backward onto an outside edge.

2 Keep moving along on the outside edge. The left side of your body should be rotated back and the free leg is out in front.

Start to cross this leg over your other leg.

Skating backward

Like forward skating, it is very important that you stand correctly over your skates when you skate backward. You can stand toward the front of the blades, but not on the toe picks. Try to center your weight.

Feet first

1 Start with your toes together and both feet on their inside edges.

2 Lift up your right foot and take it back about 6 in (15 cm).

3 Place the right foot back on the ice. Keep your toes turned in.

4 Lift your left foot and take it back about 6 in (15 cm).

5 Repeat these moves until your skates are gliding backward.

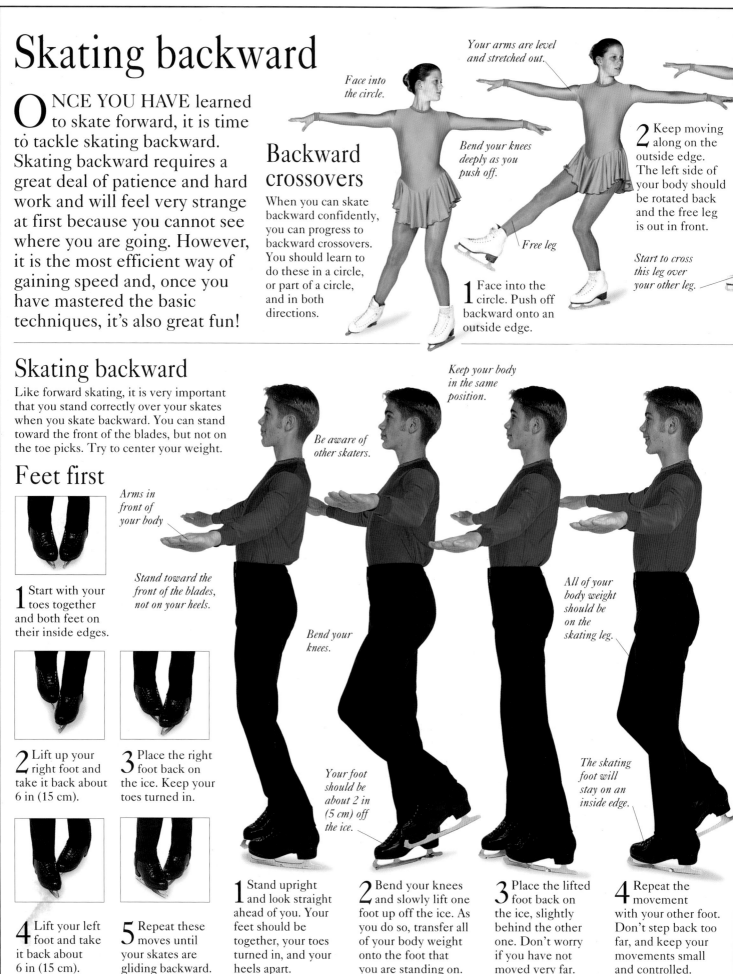

Arms in front of your body

Stand toward the front of the blades, not on your heels.

Be aware of other skaters.

Keep your body in the same position.

Bend your knees.

Your foot should be about 2 in (5 cm) off the ice.

All of your body weight should be on the skating leg.

The skating foot will stay on an inside edge.

1 Stand upright and look straight ahead of you. Your feet should be together, your toes turned in, and your heels apart.

2 Bend your knees and slowly lift one foot up off the ice. As you do so, transfer all of your body weight onto the foot that you are standing on.

3 Place the lifted foot back on the ice, slightly behind the other one. Don't worry if you have not moved very far.

4 Repeat the movement with your other foot. Don't step back too far, and keep your movements small and controlled.

3 Start to cross your extended right leg over in front of your left leg. Make sure you keep your body weight leaning into the circle.

Keep all your body weight on your skating leg.

Keep your arms stretched out to help you balance.

Your feet should be crossed.

Inside edge

4 Transfer your body weight onto your front (right) leg. The right skate should be on an inside edge.

Bend the new skating leg.

5 Start to extend your left leg. Hold your body in the same position throughout the movement.

Keep your upper body toward the center of the circle.

Bend the knee of your skating leg very deeply.

Keep looking in the direction you are traveling.

6 Bend your right leg and extend the left leg to complete the crossover. Close your feet and repeat the steps.

Backward stroking

Stroking is another name for pushing, and backward stroking is simply a continuation of backward skating. It is a great way to build up confidence and speed on the ice and to develop body weight control.

1 Begin in the start position, bend your knees, and push off with the inside edge of your right foot.

Keep your arms level throughout, with your palms facing downward.

Glide on one foot for as long as possible to help your balance.

5 Continue until you are gliding backward smoothly. Try counting as you change feet, increasing the time between changes until you feel comfortable.

2 After the push, stretch your right leg to the front and turn your foot out.

Your free side should be slightly forward.

Turn your right foot out.

Your weight is on your left leg.

Your skating side should be slightly back.

Hold the position for a few seconds, close your feet, and repeat the movements with your other leg.

Backward dips

This exercise makes you work hard at bending really low while skating backward. Like forward dips (see page 17), you have to bend your knees and ankles very deeply to get all the way down without falling.

1 Dips are easier if you can build up quite a lot of speed, so with your feet close together, start to skate backward, and then gradually bring your feet together.

2 As you start to bend your knees, bring both arms forward, and cross your hands. Don't lean back!

Keep your back as straight as possible.

Bend both knees deeply.

3 Bend all the way down, stretch out your arms and use them to push as far forward as you can.

Lu Chen

Chinese Olympic medalist Lu Chen uses her whole body to express the music. Here, she is skating a beautiful backward move on inside edges.

Keep your head up and avoid leaning back.

Edges

UNDERNEATH EACH skate blade is a hollow with an edge on either side. Edges are the foundation of ice skating. Every movement, spin, or jump that you perform on the ice will be done on an inside edge, an outside edge, or both. Edges allow you to skate curves and circles, often at great speed, and, if you can master them, also show that you have good control and balance.

Forward outside edge

The edge on the outside of your skates is the one that you will use the most. However, this edge is also the harder edge to hold, and most beginners stand on their inside edge, which is more comfortable and feels safer. With practice, you should find that you are able to control both your inside and outside edges, whether you are skating forward or backward.

1 Begin with both heels together and bend your knees deeply.

Your free side is slightly back.

Place your skating foot on the outside edge.

Make sure the skating side of your body is forward.

↗ **On the edge**
Any move that involves edges must be exactly executed, or else the move will be incorrect.

Get ready to skate in a different direction.

Start to take your left arm back and bring your right arm forward.

7 At this point in the circle, gradually start to change the position of your arms and shoulders.

8 At the final point in the circle, shift your body weight as you prepare to change feet and skate a new circle.

Stay on the outside edge.

6 Always look where you are going as you skate around the curve.

Extend your free leg to the front.

Your skating leg should be bent, not stiff.

Keep your body relaxed.

Finding your edges
If you stand with both feet slightly apart, you can feel where the inside and outside edges are by pressing onto the inside of your blades, then onto the outside of your blades.

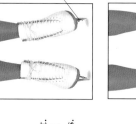

The inside edges face each other.

The outside edges are on the outside of each blade.

Inside edge
When you stand on both feet, the inside edge is the one that faces the opposite foot. Push your feet inward onto your inside edges.

Outside edge
When your feet are together, the outside edge is the one that faces away from the opposite foot. Practice pushing both feet over onto your outside edges.

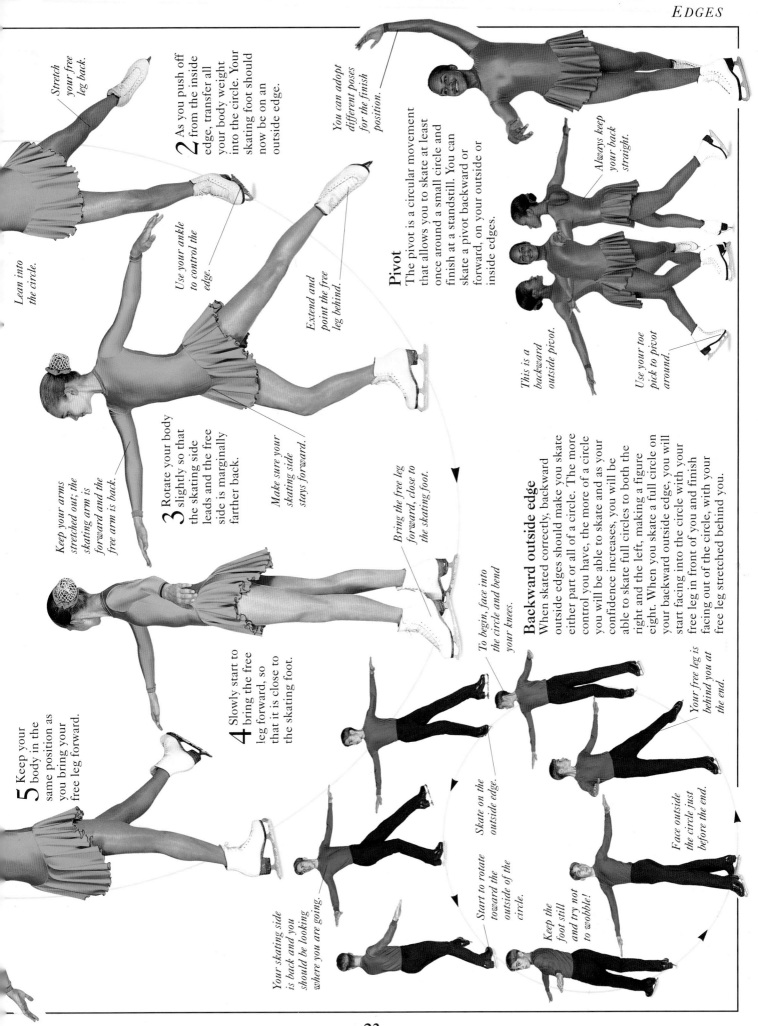

Stretch your free leg back.

2 As you push off from the inside edge, transfer all your body weight into the circle. Your skating foot should now be on an outside edge.

You can adopt different poses for the finish position.

Lean into the circle.

Use your ankle to control the edge.

Extend and point the free leg behind.

Pivot

The pivot is a circular movement that allows you to skate at least once around a small circle and finish at a standstill. You can skate a pivot backward or forward, on your outside or inside edges.

Always keep your back straight.

Keep your arms stretched out; the skating arm is forward and the free arm is back.

3 Rotate your body slightly so that the skating side leads and the free side is marginally farther back.

Make sure your skating side stays forward.

This is a backward outside pivot.

Use your toe pick to pivot around.

Bring the free leg forward, close to the skating foot.

Slowly start to bring the free leg forward, so that it is close to the skating foot.

4 Slowly start to bring the free leg forward, so that it is close to the skating foot.

To begin, face into the circle and bend your knees.

Backward outside edge

When skated correctly, backward outside edges should make you skate either part or all of a circle. The more control you have, the more of a circle you will be able to skate and as your confidence increases, you will be able to skate full circles to both the right and the left, making a figure eight. When you skate a full circle on your backward outside edge, you will start facing into the circle with your free leg in front of you and finish facing out of the circle, with your free leg stretched behind you.

Your free leg is behind you at the end.

5 Keep your body in the same position as you bring your free leg forward.

Your skating side is back and you should be looking where you are going.

Skate on the outside edge.

Start to rotate toward the outside of the circle.

Keep the foot still and try not to wobble!

Face outside the circle just before the end.

Turns

ONCE YOU HAVE mastered skating forward and backward, you will need to learn how to turn from forward to backward. There are many different turns, such as the three-turn, the mohawk, the choctaw, the bracket, the counter, and the rocker. Every turn must be done without scratching, should flow easily, and must be skated on the correct edges. You need tremendous control of your hips, shoulders, and body weight.

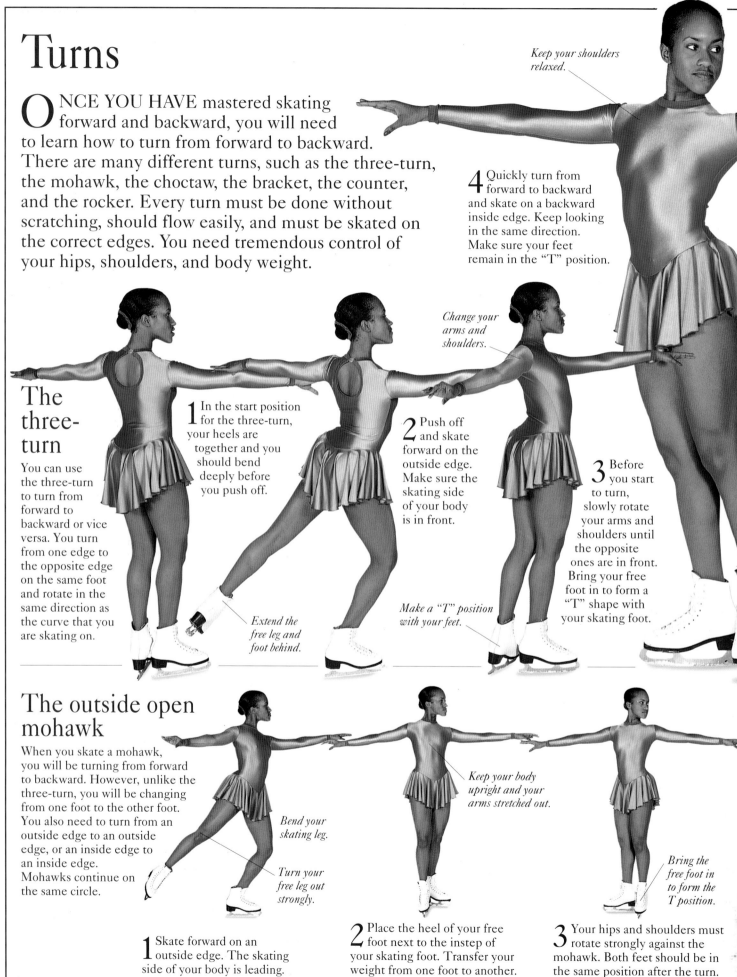

Keep your shoulders relaxed.

4 Quickly turn from forward to backward and skate on a backward inside edge. Keep looking in the same direction. Make sure your feet remain in the "T" position.

Change your arms and shoulders.

The three-turn

You can use the three-turn to turn from forward to backward or vice versa. You turn from one edge to the opposite edge on the same foot and rotate in the same direction as the curve that you are skating on.

1 In the start position for the three-turn, your heels are together and you should bend deeply before you push off.

Extend the free leg and foot behind.

2 Push off and skate forward on the outside edge. Make sure the skating side of your body is in front.

Make a "T" position with your feet.

3 Before you start to turn, slowly rotate your arms and shoulders until the opposite ones are in front. Bring your free foot in to form a "T" shape with your skating foot.

The outside open mohawk

When you skate a mohawk, you will be turning from forward to backward. However, unlike the three-turn, you will be changing from one foot to the other foot. You also need to turn from an outside edge to an outside edge, or an inside edge to an inside edge. Mohawks continue on the same circle.

Bend your skating leg.

Turn your free leg out strongly.

1 Skate forward on an outside edge. The skating side of your body is leading.

Keep your body upright and your arms stretched out.

2 Place the heel of your free foot next to the instep of your skating foot. Transfer your weight from one foot to another.

Bring the free foot in to form the T position.

3 Your hips and shoulders must rotate strongly against the mohawk. Both feet should be in the same position after the turn.

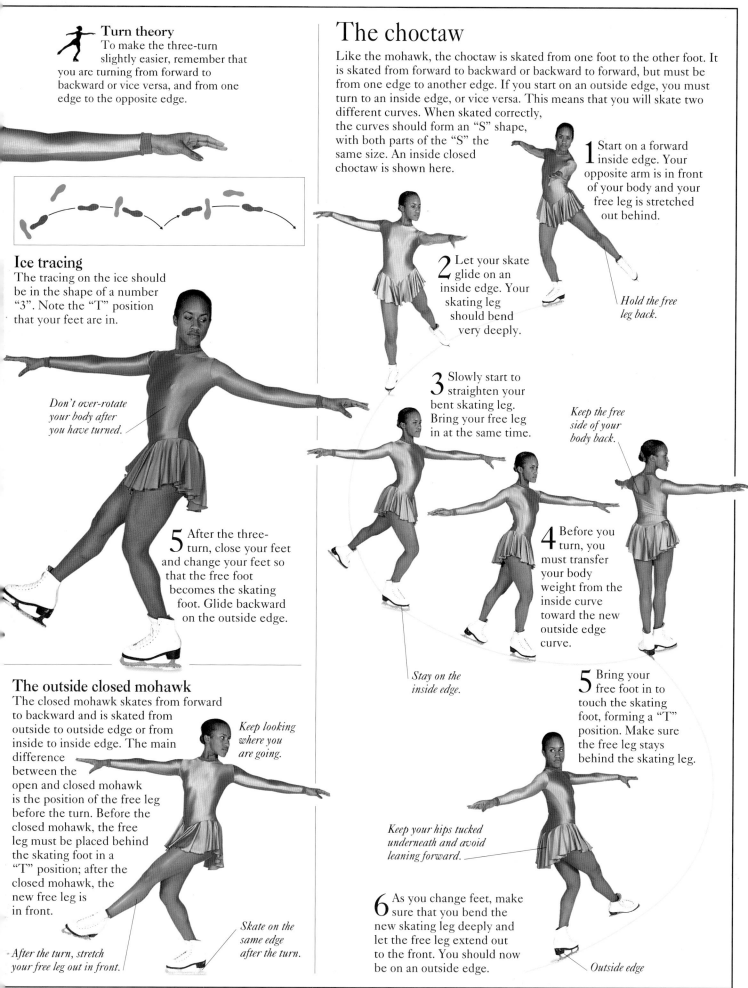

Turn theory
To make the three-turn slightly easier, remember that you are turning from forward to backward or vice versa, and from one edge to the opposite edge.

The choctaw
Like the mohawk, the choctaw is skated from one foot to the other foot. It is skated from forward to backward or backward to forward, but must be from one edge to another edge. If you start on an outside edge, you must turn to an inside edge, or vice versa. This means that you will skate two different curves. When skated correctly, the curves should form an "S" shape, with both parts of the "S" the same size. An inside closed choctaw is shown here.

1 Start on a forward inside edge. Your opposite arm is in front of your body and your free leg is stretched out behind.

Hold the free leg back.

2 Let your skate glide on an inside edge. Your skating leg should bend very deeply.

Ice tracing
The tracing on the ice should be in the shape of a number "3". Note the "T" position that your feet are in.

3 Slowly start to straighten your bent skating leg. Bring your free leg in at the same time.

Keep the free side of your body back.

Don't over-rotate your body after you have turned.

4 Before you turn, you must transfer your body weight from the inside curve toward the new outside edge curve.

5 After the three-turn, close your feet and change your feet so that the free foot becomes the skating foot. Glide backward on the outside edge.

Stay on the inside edge.

5 Bring your free foot in to touch the skating foot, forming a "T" position. Make sure the free leg stays behind the skating leg.

The outside closed mohawk
The closed mohawk skates from forward to backward and is skated from outside to outside edge or from inside to inside edge. The main difference between the open and closed mohawk is the position of the free leg before the turn. Before the closed mohawk, the free leg must be placed behind the skating foot in a "T" position; after the closed mohawk, the new free leg is in front.

Keep looking where you are going.

Keep your hips tucked underneath and avoid leaning forward.

6 As you change feet, make sure that you bend the new skating leg deeply and let the free leg extend out to the front. You should now be on an outside edge.

After the turn, stretch your free leg out in front.

Skate on the same edge after the turn.

Outside edge

Jumping on ice 1

WATCHING A SKATER jump into the air, and land perfectly at speed is one of the most exciting aspects of figure skating. Each jump has a different takeoff position, but all jumps land on the backward outside edge of the skate. They range from a half rotation in the air to a massive four rotations, and you can rotate in a clockwise or a counter clockwise direction. Always learn the correct techniques from a qualified coach.

The bunny hop

The first jump you will learn is the bunny hop. It has a forward takeoff and no rotation in the air. The bunny hop helps you to coordinate your arms, legs, and body weight while you jump. It also helps to develop good rhythm, timing, and confidence.

Extend your left arm out comfortably behind you.

Your right arm comes back as you prepare to jump.

1 Glide forward on your left leg. Make sure this leg is bent strongly. Your right arm should be out in front.

2 Bring your right leg and left arm forward as you start to jump up.

Start to push upward with this leg.

The three jump

Also called the waltz jump, the three jump has one half rotation in the air. You begin by skating forward on one leg and finish on the other leg skating backward. Both your takeoff and landing must be on an outside edge.

This position is the same as the start position for the salchow.

1 Skate a few backward crossovers and then stand on a backward outside edge on your right leg. Stretch your left leg out behind you.

2 Keeping the left arm in front, bring both feet back together so that your heels are touching. Bend your knees.

3 Step from backward to forward onto your left leg, bend your knees, and get on an outside edge. Put your arms behind your body slightly.

Bring both arms behind your body slightly.

4 As you start to jump up, bring your right leg and both arms forward at the same time. Keep your head up.

Lean forward slightly in the air.

Your left arm is back.

Your right arm comes forward as soon as you land.

Your left leg is stretched out behind you.

3 Make sure you land on the toe rake of your right foot, with your left leg stretched out behind.

4 As soon as you have landed on the toe rake of your right foot, change feet. Glide on your left foot and change your arms back again. In this position, you are ready to start again.

Use the toe rake of your right foot when you land.

Change your feet very quickly.

Takeoff

The takeoff for the three jump, shown here by Surya Bonaly, must be very explosive. Surya shows exactly how important a powerful takeoff is. She looks really relaxed, controlled, and strong, all at the same time. Remember that you should always look up when jumping, not down.

Bring your left arm in front slightly to stop your body rotating too much.

6 Before you land on your right leg, open your arms very strongly to help stop the rotation. Take your left arm forward.

7 You should be on your right leg on an outside edge when you land. Your left leg should be behind you and your left arm is slightly in front. Bend your landing leg strongly and hold the landing position for as long as possible.

5 When you are in the air, keep both arms across your body. Stretch your legs downward and keep them apart.

🤸 **Safe landings** Practice the landing position off ice without your skates on. This will help to develop your strength and improve your balance.

Bend the skating leg strongly when you land.

Point your toes downward.

Land on your toe rake and then skate backward on an outside edge.

Jumping on ice 2

MAKING EVERYTHING look effortless and easy is the magic of jumping on ice. Learning to control every move, no matter how small, is really important. Bad habits developed at this stage will be difficult to iron out later, when you will want to learn double, triple, and even quadruple jumps. This section deals with the salchow jump, which is more difficult than the three jump. The salchow has a backward takeoff from an inside edge. You must have lots of control of the backward inside edge if your jump is to be a good one.

The salchow

This jump is named after the Swede Ulrich Salchow, who was World Champion 10 times between 1900–1911. It has a backward take-off from a backward inside edge, one rotation in the air, and a landing on a backward outside edge. At all times during the salchow you should keep your shoulders and hips level. Dropping the free side of the body is a common mistake and could lead to a fall on landing.

Look where you are going before the three turn.

3 Change your feet and get ready to turn a three turn (see page 24). This will take you to a backward position.

4 Stretch your right leg out behind you and your left arm in front.

1 Build up speed by skating backward crossovers and then glide on the backward outside edge of the right leg. Extend the left leg behind you.

2 Bend your knees as you step from forward to backward.

You should be on a backward inside edge.

Safe landings
Practice the landing position off ice without your skates on. This will help to develop your strength and improve your balance.

Triple salchow
To accomplish a triple salchow, like the one in the picture, takes a lot of practice and a great deal of nerve. World Champion Maria Butryskaya here demonstrates how to rotate very quickly in the air by pulling both arms strongly in toward the body, and keeping the free leg crossed tightly in front during the jump. This will allow Maria to rotate very quickly in the air. She keeps her head up too!

This mid-air position is the same as for the three jump.

5 Jump up, bringing your right arm and leg forward.

6 Your arms should be close to your body and your legs are stretched apart.

Hold the landing position for as long as possible.

At the point of takeoff, you must jump up and over your toe rake.

7 When you land, remember to bend your right leg and keep your back and head up.

Advanced jumps 1

THIS SECTION concentrates on the more advanced single jumps. From the single jumps, you can progress to double jumps and eventually triple jumps. There are also combination jumps, which involve linking two together, such as the three jump and the loop jump. Whatever level you attempt, remember that in order to perform it well, you need to develop a good sense of timing.

The loop jump

This jump takes off from a backward outside edge and lands on the backward outside edge of the same foot. It has one rotation in the air.

Left arm leads.

1 Use backward crossovers to pick up some speed. You will be jumping from your right leg and landing on your right leg.

2 Stand on the outside edge of your right foot, ready to jump. Keep your shoulders level.

3 Bend strongly and push up into the air. Jump over the toe rake. Quickly bring your arms in toward your body.

The flip

Also known as a toe salchow, the flip has one full rotation in the air. It has a backward inside edge take off and is assisted by the toe rake of the free foot. As with all jumps, you should concentrate on controlling your body movements throughout the jump. All jumps must have good timing and rhythm. Counting to yourself in your head can help achieve this.

Head up! Look where you are going.

Avoid lifting your shoulders.

Think and skate straight.

Bend the knee and ankle of your skating leg strongly.

1 Begin by skating forward on the outside edge of your left foot. Your right leg is forward. The right toe must be pointed.

2 Stay on your left leg, but slowly start to bring your feet together and change the position of your arms and shoulders. Try to keep the jump heading in a straight line.

3 Use the right toe rake to push with and then stretch the right leg behind. Your arms should now have changed fully, so that you are ready to turn a three turn.

Avoid stiff landings; always bend your knee when you land.

Stretch the free leg back.

Bring both arms in toward the body as you rotate.

Do not lean backward.

Keep your back upright.

Push up hard into the air.

Your skating foot should be on a strong outside edge.

4 When you are in the air, your arms must be close to your body. Open them just before you land.

5 Land on your right foot on an outside edge. Bend your right knee and glide backward.

4 Turn a three turn (see page 24) which will take you onto the backward inside edge. Stay on the same foot. Keep practicing this three turn to help you master the control.

5 Bend the left leg very strongly and reach back with the right leg. Tap the right toe rake into the ice. Keep your back upright.

6 As you push up into the air from your left leg, transfer your body weight onto the right leg and you will jump up. Bring both arms toward your body.

7 Land on a strong outside edge. Bend the skating leg and stretch the free leg back.

Advanced jumps 2

THE KEY TO GOOD jumping is how well and often you practice. The best skaters in the world will practice the jumps shown in this book every day and transform them into really advanced jumps, such as the triple salchow or the triple lutz. Remember, the more precisely you do the jump, the easier you will find it to advance. It is great fun trying the more advanced jumps for the first time; but if they do not work, keep trying! You need determination to be a great skater.

The lutz

This jump is rather difficult to learn because it is the only one to jump against the takeoff edge. The lutz must take off from a backward outside edge; try to avoid changing edge as you take off.

Right arm is forward, left arm is back.

At this point you must feel well balanced.

1 Start by skating backward crossovers in a clockwise direction. Stand on the left leg on an outside edge. Keep looking ahead.

Practice the backward outside edge without jumping at first.

The toe loop

Like the flip, the toe loop, or cherry flip, also has one rotation in the air. Take off from a backward outside edge and land on a backward outside edge. During takeoff, avoid skating on your toe rake.

No leaning in; stand strongly.

Right leg and left arm in front.

Stay balanced at this point.

Never rush the arm movement.

Reach back with this leg.

1 Begin on the left foot on a forward inside edge. Your left arm is forward and your right leg is in front.

2 Stay on an inside edge as you change onto your right foot. Keep your arms in the same position and bend strongly as you push.

3 Turn an inside three turn so that you are skating backward. Reach back with the left leg ready to tap the toe rake into the ice.

4 As you tap the ice, let your right leg continue gliding back until your feet are together. This will happen very quickly.

Keep your right arm back before takeoff.

2 Slowly change your arms and take the free leg behind. Bend the skating leg as you do this. Tap the toe into the ice as you jump to your left against the takeoff edge.

Tap this toe into the ice.

Triple lutz

American and world skating champion Michelle Kwan demonstrates the triple lutz. You can see how compact Michelle is in the air as she rotates three times. Once in the air, the trick is to rotate very quickly, by pulling your arms in toward your body to increase rotational speed. To stop the rotation, you open your arms; this will result in a smooth and flowing landing.

Both arms close to the body.

Note how all jump landings are the same.

Rotation
The stronger and quicker your arms are brought toward your body, the quicker you will rotate.

Jump up from this toe.

Land toe first, then a flowing outside edge.

As soon as you land, take the free leg behind.

5 Jump up from the toe of the left foot and at the same time, bring your arms and right leg forward.

6 The mid-air position is the same as for the three jump. Make sure you are balanced during the jump.

7 Open both arms and take your left leg slightly to the front, ready to land.

8 When you land, quickly take the free leg behind and make sure that you bend the skating leg very strongly.

Spinning on ice

S PINNING IS ONE of the most important and fascinating elements of free skating. Experienced skaters can rotate dozens of times and reach amazing speeds when they spin. However, spinning on ice is not easy, and when you first start to learn you will feel very dizzy. This is normal, and as your technique and balance improve, these feelings will disappear. Skaters usually spin in one direction (either clockwise or counter clockwise) and on one foot. Try an upright spin first, followed by a sit spin, then a camel, or parallel, spin.

Your arms and fingers should be elegant.

One-foot upright spin

This spin is probably the most important, because once you have mastered it, other variations become possible. Every spin begins in the same way, and the first three stages of the camel spin (below) outline the entry instructions for all the other spins.

Extend your free leg strongly to the side.

Place the free foot next to the spinning knee.

Always spin on the ball of your foot.

1 After you have turned a three-turn so that you are skating backward, you will be spinning on the backward inside edge of your right skate.

2 Find your balance and slowly bring the extended leg toward the spinning leg.

3 Bring both arms in to your body to make you spin much faster. Always keep your head up and your shoulders and hips level while you are spinning.

Skate in a clockwise direction.

Keep the left shoulder and arm in front.

Camel spin

In a camel spin, you keep your free leg behind you, instead of bringing it forward. It is the slowest of all the spins and looks rather like a spinning arabesque or spiral.

Skate on a very strong forward outside edge for at least half a circle.

Spin on a backward inside edge.

5 Keep the free leg well stretched behind you and lift it as high as possible into a spiral position.

1 Skate several backward crossovers and hold the final crossover. Bring the left arm forward across the body.

2 Step from a backward inside edge to a forward outside edge. Your skating leg must be well bent.

3 Let the outside edge come around for at least half a circle before turning a very quick three-turn.

4 After the three-turn, you will be facing the opposite direction and spinning on a backward inside edge.

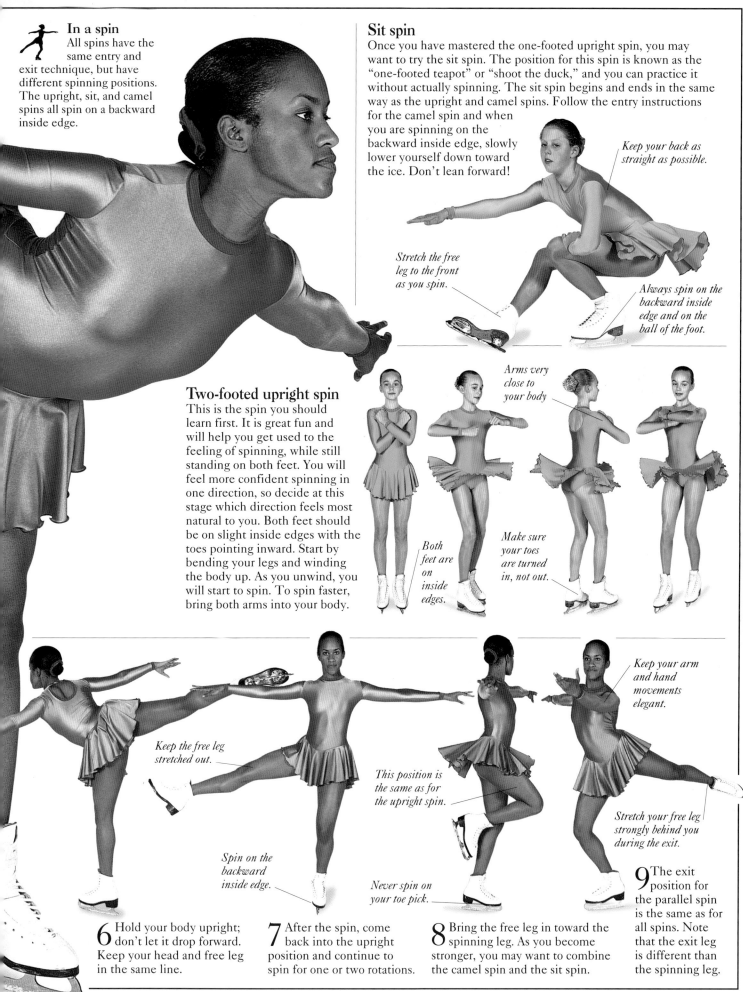

In a spin

All spins have the same entry and exit technique, but have different spinning positions. The upright, sit, and camel spins all spin on a backward inside edge.

Sit spin

Once you have mastered the one-footed upright spin, you may want to try the sit spin. The position for this spin is known as the "one-footed teapot" or "shoot the duck," and you can practice it without actually spinning. The sit spin begins and ends in the same way as the upright and camel spins. Follow the entry instructions for the camel spin and when you are spinning on the backward inside edge, slowly lower yourself down toward the ice. Don't lean forward!

Keep your back as straight as possible.

Stretch the free leg to the front as you spin.

Always spin on the backward inside edge and on the ball of the foot.

Two-footed upright spin

This is the spin you should learn first. It is great fun and will help you get used to the feeling of spinning, while still standing on both feet. You will feel more confident spinning in one direction, so decide at this stage which direction feels most natural to you. Both feet should be on slight inside edges with the toes pointing inward. Start by bending your legs and winding the body up. As you unwind, you will start to spin. To spin faster, bring both arms into your body.

Arms very close to your body

Both feet are on inside edges.

Make sure your toes are turned in, not out.

Keep the free leg stretched out.

Keep your arm and hand movements elegant.

Spin on the backward inside edge.

This position is the same as for the upright spin.

Never spin on your toe pick.

Stretch your free leg strongly behind you during the exit.

6 Hold your body upright; don't let it drop forward. Keep your head and free leg in the same line.

7 After the spin, come back into the upright position and continue to spin for one or two rotations.

8 Bring the free leg in toward the spinning leg. As you become stronger, you may want to combine the camel spin and the sit spin.

9 The exit position for the parallel spin is the same as for all spins. Note that the exit leg is different than the spinning leg.

Ice dancing

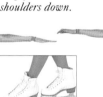

Keep the right arm forward.

Remember to bend this leg strongly after the run.

Turn your free leg out.

FOR MANY PEOPLE, ice dancing is the most attractive form of ice skating. There are two parts to ice dancing. The compulsory dances consist of prescribed steps and patterns performed to music with a specific rhythm, such as the foxtrot or waltz. In the free dance, skaters are allowed to choose their own steps and music.

Forward runs

A forward run looks a bit like a crossover, but the crucial difference is that your feet must not cross over.

1 From the basic start position on your left leg, get on an outside edge and push your left hip forward.

2 Slowly bring your right leg forward. Place it on the ice on an inside edge, directly in front of the left.

3 After the run, push with the outside edge of the left skate and bend the right leg strongly.

Backward runs

Like forward runs, backward runs involve a series of steps running clockwise or counter clockwise. The free leg is taken behind the skating foot, but again, your feet must not cross. Instead, place the new skating foot in line with the old foot.

Always look in the direction you are going.

Skating leg

1 Start on the outside edge, bend your left leg strongly and extend your right leg to the front.

The right leg becomes the new skating leg.

2 Take your right leg back so that it is very close to the left foot and then place it on the ice behind the left foot.

Keep your shoulders down.

Feet first
Always keep your feet in line; never cross them.

Make sure your left hip is back.

3 You should now be on a backward inside edge. Keep looking where you are going.

Open chassé

The word "chassé" is from a French word that means "to chase," which is what the feet do in this step sequence. As in all ice dance steps, you must bring the free foot close to the skating foot and keep it near the ice.

The skating foot is on an outside edge.

Lift the foot to ankle height. The blade is parallel with the ice.

1 Push off onto an outside edge and bring both feet together. Place the free foot next to the skating foot on an inside edge.

2 Keeping the feet together, quickly lift the skating foot up off the ice. Place the free foot back on the ice, ready to start again.

Closed chassé

A closed chassé consists of two steps from an outside edge to an inside edge, and involves placing the free foot on the ice, crossed behind the skating foot. Keep the skating side of your body forward.

Place the free foot on the ice on an inside edge.

1 From a basic skating position, cross the free foot fully behind the skating foot.

2 After the closed chassé, extend the free foot forward. Bring the feet together and repeat.

The skating side of your body is forward all the time.

The skating foot is on an outside edge.

Forward cross roll

A cross roll is a movement in which you skate on the outside edges of your skates, moving from outside edge to outside edge. Done correctly, this will make you skate two perfect half circles. Control of your hips, shoulders, and body weight during cross rolls is crucial. A good tip is to keep your hips and shoulders in line.

Keep your body upright.

Start to bring the left arm forward.

Your left leg is the skating leg and it should be on an outside edge.

Use the outside edge of your back foot to push away.

1 Start on your left leg, on an outside edge. Your left hip should be leading, and your right arm and shoulder are forward.

2 Bring the right leg forward, very close to the left foot. Take it across the left foot and place it on the ice on an outside edge.

3 After the cross roll, bend the new skating leg strongly and stretch the free leg back.

Feet first
Always skate from outside to outside edge. The back foot pushes away using the outside edge.

Backward cross roll

The best way to perfect your cross roll technique is to skate several of them together. Try skating the full length of the rink, picking up speed as you go. Always skate from outside edge to outside edge; never skate on the inside edge.

Skating leg

Free leg

1 From the basic start position, take the free leg and place it behind the skating foot, on an outside edge.

2 Bend strongly onto the outside edge of the left leg. This is now the skating leg. Extend the other leg in front.

Ice tracing
The two half-circle tracings left on the ice by a cross roll look like an "S."

Positions and holds

The three main ice dance positions are the Waltz hold, the Foxtrot hold, and the Kilian hold. These positions are used in the compulsory dance sections. During the free dance section, skaters can invent their own, new and different, holds.

The female's elbow should be forward.

The Kilian hold
For the Kilian hold, the male takes the female's left hand with his left hand, and the female places her right hand on top of his right hand.

The turned-out pushing foot should be on an inside edge, ready to push off.

The Foxtrot hold
Both skaters skate in the same direction during the Foxtrot hold. The female partner stands on the right and slightly in front of the male.

The Waltz hold
Skaters must maintain the Waltz position at all times during the Waltz. One skater skates backward while the other skates forward. The shoulders and hips should be parallel at all times.

Perfection on ice
There is total freedom of expression during this thrilling free dance move. Anjelika Krylova and Oleg Ovsyannikov are masters of ice dancing; they create many of their own moves.

Pair skating

THE SPECTACULAR lifts, throws, twists, and spins in pair skating make it the most dangerous and difficult of all the figure skating disciplines, as well as the most exciting. Pair skating combines elements of ice dancing, free skating, and compulsory dances but is much faster and more complicated. One of the most important issues for anyone wishing to take up pair skating is the choice of a partner. Ideally, you should look for someone of a similar standard, age, and style to yourself. Both you and your partner must be excellent free skaters, and you should seek professional coaching before you attempt any of the moves.

Vadim has to turn very quickly while still supporting his partner.

Evgenia Shishkova and Vadim Naumov
The 1994 World Pair Skating Champions are from St. Petersburg, Russia. The amazing one-handed overhead lift shown here is called a star lift. Vadim holds Evgenia above his head with ease; his raised arm is locked, giving Evgenia total support in the air.

An overhead lift
The Russian pair demonstrates another overhead lift, in which Evgenia is completely horizontal and Vadim has to turn as he skates along at great speed. This is extremely difficult and dangerous.

Natalia Mishkuteniok and Artur Dmitriev
Russian skaters Natalia and Artur won the 1992 Olympic gold medal in Albertville, France. They are extremely dramatic skaters. Here, they are performing a thrilling and dangerous movement, in which Natalia is balanced on Artur's back while Artur skates a forward outside spiral. Even in this position, the skater's arms and legs align beautifully and everything matches perfectly.

Maria and Andrei's power, grace, and elegance make their movements look easy.

Maria Eltsova and Andrei Bushkov

Russians Maria and Andrei are the 1997 European Champions and have won many other skating championships. In pair skating, the skaters must not only be able to jump, lift, and throw, but they must also be able to spin together. Here, Maria and Andrei are performing a sit spin together. Maria is spinning on a backward outside edge, while Andrei is spinning on a backward inside edge.

Natasha Kuchiki and Todd Sand

The death spiral is one of the most elegant moves in pair skating. Former American pair Natasha and Todd are shown here performing an impressive backward inside death spiral. Natasha is skating on her left leg and on a very deep backward inside edge. The death spiral can also be skated on a forward inside edge or on a backward outside edge. The male partner will always skate a backward outside pivot and must bend very deeply into the pivot.

All pair skating moves must be well timed if they are to work effectively.

Off the ice
Pair skaters should practice off the ice to develop their lifts and moves before they attempt them on the ice.

Mandy Woetzel and Ingo Steur

The 1997 World Pair Skating Champions, Germans Mandy and Ingo are performing an elegant backward outside death spiral. The death spiral allows skaters to combine graceful, fluid movements with dramatic, acrobatic ones. Mandy's head is almost touching the ice as she skates a very strong backward outside edge. Ingo is performing a backward outside pivot and using all his strength to support Mandy during the move.

Mandy stretches through her free leg to create resistance with her partner.

Taking it further

ONCE YOU HAVE discovered the joys of ice skating, you may wish to explore some of the many other aspects of the sport. This section will give you some ideas about how you can develop your skating skills further. You could try speed skating, ice hockey, or curling, for example, or you may consider a career in figure skating as a coach or a show skater. Whatever you choose, ice skating offers a vast choice of things to do and enjoy while keeping fit and healthy. Enjoy it!

In competition
One of the main thrills of ice skating lies in competing. The sheer elation that follows a brilliant performance can be clearly seen here on the face of American Olympic gold medalist, Tara Lipinski. All skaters have to endure the nerve-wracking wait for the judge's marks in the "kiss-and-cry" box, surrounded by flowers and their coaches.

Tara Lipinski, at 15, is the youngest skater ever to win Olympic gold in ladies figure skating.

Coaching
Competitive skaters spend a lot of time with their coaches. Your coach will give you advice on all aspects of ice skating. He or she will also plan your training program and give you lots of confidence to perform well.

Anjelika Krylova and Oleg Ovsyannikov

Pasha Grishur and Evgeny Platov

Winning medals
Being selected for the Olympic Games, which are held every four years, is an ambition that every young skater dreams about. At the 1998 Nagano Olympics in Japan, Russians Pasha Grishur and Evgeny Platov won the gold medal, Russians Anjelika Krylova and Oleg Ovsyannikov won the silver, and French skaters Marina Anissina and Gwendal Peizerat won the bronze.

Marina Anissina and Gwendal Peizerat

Precision skating
In 1990, a new skating discipline was introduced, called precision skating. Precision skaters skate in different group formations, performing steps to music. All the moves must be performed with great accuracy and the group should skate as one body. This type of skating often appeals to people who prefer to skate as part of a group, rather than individually.

Holiday On Ice
The glamour of skating in an ice show appeals to many skaters. Ice companies tour the world with the show and often have famous names in the lead roles. One of the most famous ice shows is "Holiday On Ice," shown above.

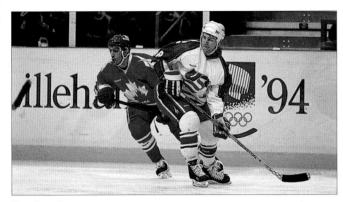

Ice hockey

This fast-moving, demanding game is one of the most popular in the world. Two teams of six skaters play for three 20-minute periods. Players wear thick protective clothing and carry wooden hockey sticks. The winning team is the one that scores the most goals with a weighted puck.

Curling

The game of curling is thought to have originated in Scotland or the Netherlands about 400 years ago. Two teams of four players compete on a level sheet of ice. The players slide heavy curling stones made of granite toward a circle at the far end of the ice, called a house. Players often sweep the ice in front of the stone with a broom to make the stone travel farther.

Speed skating

In this fast, competitive sport, skaters can reach speeds of up to 34 mph (56 kph)! Speed skating began centuries ago, and was traditionally held outdoors. Some of today's speed skating events are still held out of doors. Skaters wear special boots with longer, single-edged blades to help them start quickly and maintain high speeds throughout a race, and close-fitting lycra clothing to reduce wind resistance. To be successful, a speed skater must be strong and have excellent balance, rhythm, and drive.

Speed skaters keep their back straight and lean forward from the waist. Their bodies should be relaxed and flexible.

Smooth, powerful strokes make speed skating a very graceful sport.

Outdoor rinks

In cities such as Toronto, in Canada, large areas are flooded during the winter months and made into huge outdoor ice rinks. Skaters of all ages take to the ice, making skating one of the most popular sports in Canada.

Skating outdoors is not only fun, but great exercise, too! Always remember to dress warmly.

Nature's ice rinks

In a few countries with exceptionally cold winter weather, lakes, canals, and even the sea will freeze! Many people skate on these frozen areas as a fun way of getting around and exercising. However, when skating on any kind of natural ice, you should always take great care. The ice may not only be thin, but can also be covered with leaves and branches, making the surface rough and the skating hazardous. Always skate with a reliable adult, never on your own; and if the ice looks thin, do not skate on it.

Glossary

You may be unfamiliar with many of the terms used by ice skaters. Some of the more common ones are listed below.

A

Axis An imaginary line running through the center of the skater, around which the skater moves, jumps, and spins.

B

Blade guards Plastic or rubber blade protectors.

Bracket A one-foot turn from forward to backward or vice versa, from outside to inside or inside to outside, turning against the curve.

Bunny hop A jumping movement without rotation, jumping and landing forward from the same leg, with a toe-assisted landing.

C

Chassé A two-step movement, either forward or backward and usually from outside edge to inside edge, in which the skating foot is lifted slightly off the ice and placed next to the new skating foot.

Check To check a turn is to fully stop the rotation prior to turning, and then slightly reverse the rotation before turning.

Choctaw A turn from forward to backward or vice versa, incorporating a change of feet and edge at the point of turn.

Combination jump/spin A jump or spin which involves more than one jump, or has a change of foot, and perhaps position, while spinning.

Compulsory dance A set sequence of steps skated to specific rhythms in a set hold, for example, the Waltz.

Counter A turn from forward to backward or vice versa, turning against the curve and remaining on the same edge throughout. This creates a new curve after the turn.

Crossover A movement when one foot completely crosses over the other foot to produce a gradual turn – can be skated forward or backward.

Cross rolls A series of crossed steps from outside edge to outside edge, creating a series of equal half circles.

Curling A game with two teams of four players (without ice skates), each sliding heavy stones, made of polished granite, over a smooth sheet of ice toward the center of a circle at the far end of the ice rink.

D

Death spiral A movement in pairs skating in which the male skater holds the female by the hand as he performs a backward outside pivot. The male skater uses his balance and control to support the female. The female may be skating forward or backward, on an outside or an inside edge, while spiraling around him very close to the ice, her head almost touching the ice.

Dip A move in which a skater bends both knees and lowers the body down toward the ice, while staying balanced.

E

Edge The curves skated by the blade, depending on the position of the body weight. All steps are skated on specific edges.

F

Flip (toe salchow) A jump performed from a backward inside edge, landing on a backward outside edge of the opposite leg. The flip is a toe-assisted jump at takeoff and can be performed from single through to quadruple.

Flying spin A jump followed by a spin.

Forward glide When a skater is moving forward on one foot.

Foxtrot hold A hold in ice dancing where both skaters skate in the same direction. The female stands on the right and slightly in front of the male.

Free dance A skating program devised by a dance couple, lasting for a set period of time and interpreting several different musical tempos.

Free foot/leg The foot/leg that is not actually used on the ice and skating.

G

Grind The process of sharpening skate blades. A grind varies according to the skating discipline and the skater's height and weight.

Two-footed upright spin

Parallel spin position

H
Hockey stop A method of stopping.

Hollow The space on a blade between the two edges which, according to the grind, will be deeper or shallower.

I
Inside edge The edge on the inside of the skater's foot.

K
Kilian hold A hold in ice dancing, when the male holds the female's left hand in his left hand, so her arm crosses in front of his chest. The female's right hand is placed on top of his right hand on her hip.

L
Loop jump A jump with a takeoff and landing on the same foot. The skater will takeoff and land on the backward outside edge.

Lutz jump A jump with the takeoff from a backward outside edge, and landing on the opposite leg, also on a backward outside edge. The lutz jump is a toe-assisted jump, may be rotated up to four times in the air and has counter rotation (against the natural direction of the takeoff edge).

takeoff

M
Mohawk A 180° turn from forward to backward with a change of feet. The edges remain the same throughout.

O
Outside edge The edge on the outside of the skater's foot.

P
Parallel spin (camel spin) A spin, on the backward inside edge, in which the skater assumes a horizontal spinning position, like a spiral or an arabesque. The free leg must be lifted as high as possible during the spin with both arms extended.

Pivot A circular movement, either forward or backward, on an outside or inside edge, that allows the skater to skate around the toe of the free foot at least once. The skater's body weight changes slowly from the skated edge to the toe of the free foot. The movement is generally completed at a standstill.

R
Rocker A turn skated on one foot and on the same edge, rotating naturally with the curve from forward to backward or vice versa.

Run A movement, either backward or forward, when a skater's feet alternately step clockwise and counter clockwise without crossing over.

S
Salchow A jump from a backward inside edge to the backward outside edge of the opposite leg. The salchow may rotate in the air up to four times.

Sculling A method of gliding forward, or backward, by moving both feet in and out, always on inside edges. A very strong knee action will help the skater to scull correctly.

Sit spin A spin on the backward inside edge. The skater's body is lowered toward the ice by bending the skating leg strongly. The free leg should be extended to the front, with the back and head held upright. Both arms are held close to the body to help rotate quickly.

Skating leg/foot The leg/foot that is on the ice.

Snowplow A method of stopping.

Stroke A step onto an edge that involves an increase of speed.

Stroking The usual way of skating forward.

Swing A movement in which the skater takes the free leg past the skating foot and then brings the feet together.

T
Three jump (waltz jump) A jump taking off from one leg from a forward outside edge, landing on the backward outside edge of the other leg. There is a half-turn in the air.

Three turn A one-foot turn from outside to inside or vice versa, and from forward to backward or vice versa, rotating within the circle.

Toe loop (cherry flip) The toe loop is a toe-assisted jump, taking off from the backward outside edge and landing on the backward outside edge of the same leg. The toe loop may be rotated up to four times in the air for very advanced skaters.

Toe rake (or pick) The jagged, tooth-like section at the front of a skate blade.

T stop A method of stopping.

U
Upright spin A simple upright spin will rotate on one foot on the backward inside edge, spinning around as many times as possible. The upright spin may also be skated on both feet. To spin quickly both arms should be brought very close to the body.

W
Waltz hold An ice dance hold in which one skater is skating forward while the other backward; hips and shoulders should be parallel at all times. The male skater's right hand is placed on the female's left shoulder blade, while both other hands are clasped together and extended in line with the shoulders.

Bunny hop landing

Index

Useful addresses

National Governing Body for the Sport of Figure Skating in the United States
20 First Street
Colorado Springs, CO 80906
Tel: (719) 635-5200

Ice Skating Institute
17120 North Dallas Parkway
Suite 140
Dallas, Texas 75248
Tel: (972) 735-8800
An association for recreational ice skating that organizes learn-to-skate programs.

US Olympic Training Center
1 Olympic Plaza
Colorado Springs, CO 80909
Website: www.olympic-usa.org
Tel: (719) 578-4529

International Skating Union (ISU)
Chemin de Primrose 2
1007 Lausanne
Switzerland

Skating Magazine
20 First Street
Colorado Springs, CO 80906
Tel: (719) 635-5200
Coverage of national and international figure skating.

Blades on Ice
7040 Mona Lisa Road
Tucson, Arizona 85741-2633
Tel: (520) 575-1747
Bi-monthly skating news magazine.

Canadian Figure Skating Association
#403, 1600 James Naismith Dr.
Gloucester, ON K1B 5N4
Tel: (613) 748-5635
Email: cfsa@cfsa.ca
URL: http://www.cfsa.ca/

Canadian Amateur Speed Skating Association
#312, 1600 James Naismith Dr.
Gloucester, ON K1B 5N4
Tel: (613) 748-5669
Email: ssc@speedskating-canada.ca
URL: http://www.speedskating-canada.ca

Louisa

Shellie

John

Zoia

Phillip

Adam

Acknowledgments

Dorling Kindersley would like to thank the following people
for their help in the production of this book:

Special thanks to Peter Morrissey for his technical advice and help in organizing the photo shoots; all the young ice skaters for their patience and good humor during the photography, and also their families; Celia Godsall and the staff at NISA for their involvement in the project and their advice throughout; Gary Stefan and the staff at Slough Ice Arena for their cooperation and enthusiasm; Les Westaway for supplying the ice skates; Sue Gee for making the outfits; Nichola Roberts for editorial assistance; Goldberry Broad for design assistance; Giles Powell-Smith for the jacket design.

Picture credits
The publisher would like to thank the following for their kind permission to reproduce the photographs:
Key: *l* left, *r* right, *t* top, *c* center *a* above, *b* below
Actionplus: Glyn Kirk *27tr*, DPPI *29tr*, Neil Tingle *33tr*, Chris Barry *41tr*, Richard Francis *41crb, br, 41tl*; **Allsport:** Chris Cole *10tl*, Jon Ferrey *10c*, Aubrey Washington *10cl*, Jamie Squire *40tr*, Brunckill *40cr*, Graham Chadwick *37br*; **Archive Photos:** /Hirz *11cr*; **Colorsport:** *41cl*; **Corbis-** Bettmann/UPI: *11bc*; **Mary Evans Picture Library:** *11clb, cla, bl, tr*; **Michelle Harvath:** *10bl*; **Hulton Getty:** *11c, br*; **Heinz Kluetmeier:** *10br*; **Eileen Langsley/ Supersport:** *37br, 38tr, bl, br, 39tl, b, tr, c, bl*; **National Ice Skating Association of UK Ltd:** *113c*; **Tony Stone Images:** E. N. Van Loo *41bl*; **York Archaeological Trust:** *11tl*.
Endpapers: **Sporting Pictures**;
Jacket: **Supersport Ltd/ Richard Sellers**